D0772676

LEARN
Russian
WORDS

pot
кастрюля
(kahs-TRYOO-lyah)

mother
мама
(MAH-mah)

meat
мясо
(MYA-suh)

fork
вилка
(VEEL-kuh)

knife
нож
(NOHSH)

spoon
ложка
(LOHSH-kuh)

vegetables
овощи
(OH-vah-sh'eeh)

BY M. J. YORK • ILLUSTRATED BY KATHLEEN PETELINSEK

Published by The Child's World®
1980 Lookout Drive • Mankato, MN 56003-1705
800-599-READ • www.childsworld.com

Acknowledgments
The Child's World®: Mary Berendes, Publishing Director
Translator: Ekaterina Efimenko, Language Lab Instructor in
Russian, Macalester College
The Design Lab: Design
Red Line Editorial: Editorial direction
Amnet: Production

5656 0815 04/15

ISBN 9781626873780
LCCN 2014930628

Printed in the United States of America
Mankato, MN
July, 2014
PA02217

ABOUT THE AUTHOR

M. J. York is a children's author and editor living in Minnesota. She loves learning about different people and places.

ABOUT THE ILLUSTRATOR

Kathleen Petelinsek loves to draw and paint. She also loves to travel to exotic countries where people speak foreign languages. She lives in Minnesota with her husband, two daughters, two dogs, a fluffy cat, and three chickens.

CONTENTS

Introduction to Russian

Russian is spoken in Eastern Europe and parts of Asia. It is the language of Russia and many nearby countries. At least 160 million people speak Russian. The Russian alphabet is called Cyrillic.

Russian is one of several Slavic languages. It is closely related to Ukrainian and Belorussian. Russian has several forms, including northern, southern, central, and the way it is spoken in Moscow, Russia's capital.

Russia of the 1800s is famous for its literature. Russian authors wrote many important and classic works. Some authors include Aleksandr Pushkin, Leo Tolstoy, and Anton Chekhov.

ь is called the soft sign. It does not have its own sound. It changes how you say the previous letter. The sound is clipped off or softened. It is shown with an apostrophe (') in the pronunciations in this book.

ъ is the hard sign. It separates some prefixes from the rest of the word. It makes no sound of its own. It is rarely used.

А [a] – like a in *apple*

Б [b] – like b in *boy*

В [v] – like v in *volcano*

Г [g] – like g in *gamma*

Д [d] – like d in *dog*

Е [ye] –like ye in *yes*

Ё [yo] – like yo in *New York*, always stressed

Ж [zh] – like s in *vision*, with tongue farther back

З [z] – like z in *zoo*

И [ee] – like ee in *teeth*

Й [j] – like y in *toy* or *gray*

К [k] – like k in *skit*, but without aspiration or breath

Л [l] – like l in *lamb*

М [m] – like m in *mother*

Н [n] – like n in *no*

О [o] –like a in *talk*

П [p] – like p in *pie*

Р [r] – flap r

С [s] – like s in *sail*

Т [t] – like t in *stay*, but with tongue against upper teeth

У [oo] – like oo in *foot*, with extreme lip rounding

Ф [f] – like f in *football*

Х [kh] – like ch in *Bach*

Ц [ts] – like ts in *cats*

Ч [ch] – like ch in *cheer*

Ш [sh] – like sh in *sure*, with tongue farther back

Щ [sh'] – like sh in *sheet*

Ы [y] – a sound between the a in *about* and the ee in *see*

Э [e] – like e in *set*

Ю [yoo] – like you in *you*

Я [ya] – when stressed, like ya in *yacht*

My Home
Дома
(DO-muh)

window
окно
(ak-NOH)

bathroom
ванная
(VAHN-nah-yah)

lamp
лампа
(LAHM-puh)

bedroom
спальня
(SPAHL'- nyah)

television
телевизор
(tee-lee-VEE-zuhr)

cat
кошка
(KOSH-kuh)

kitchen
кухня
(KOOKH-nyah)

living room
гостиная
(gahs-TEE-nah-yah)

sofa
диван
(dee-VAHN)

chair
стул
(STOOL)

table
стол
(STOHL)

garage
гараж
(gah-RAHSH)

car
машина
(mah-SHEE-nuh)

I live in an apartment.
Я живу в квартире.
(YA zhy-VOO V-kvahr-TEE-ryeh.)

MORE USEFUL WORDS
I live in a house.
Я живу в доме.
(YA zhy-VOO v-DOH-myeh.)

apartment
Квартира
(kvahr-TEE-ruh)

house
дом
(DOHM)

Where do you live?
Где ты живёшь?
(GDYE TY zhy-VYOSH?)

dog
собака
(sah-BAH-kah)

garden
сад
(SAHT)

In the Morning
Утром
(OO-truhm)

dresser
комод
(ka-MOT)

clock
часы
(cha-SY)

teddy bear
плюшевый
медвежонок
*(PLYOO-shy-vyj
meed-vee-ZHOH-nuhk)*

doll
кукла
(KOOK-luh)

pillow
подушка
(pa-DOOSH-kuh)

bed
кровать
(kra-VAHT')

blanket
одеяло
(ah-dee-YAH-luh)

comb
расчёска
(ras-CHYOS-kuh)

brush
щётка
(SH'OHT-kuh)

closet
шкаф для одежды
(SHKAHF DLYA ah-DYEZH-dy)

Good morning! It is seven o'clock in the morning.
Доброе утро!
Семь часов утра.
*(DOHB-rah-yeh OOT-ruh!
SYEM' cha-SOHF oot-RAH.)*

shirt
рубашка
(roo-BAHSH-kuh)

I feel awake (female).
проснулась.
(YA prahs-NOO-lahs'.)

I feel awake (male).
Я проснулся.
(YA prahs-NOOL-syah.)

dress
платье
(PLAHT'-yeh)

MORE USEFUL WORDS

I feel happy (female).
счастлива.
(YA SH'AST-lee-vuh.)

I feel happy (male).
Я счастлив.
(YA SH'AST-leef.)

I feel sad.
Мне грустно.
(MNYE GROOS-nuh.)

I feel tired (female).
устала.
(YA oos-TAH-luh.)

I feel tired (male).
Я устал.
(YA oos-TAHL.)

socks
носки
(na-SKEE)

skirt
юбка
(YOOP-kuh)

pants
штаны
(shta-NY)

shoes
туфли
(TOOF-lee)

9

At School
В школе
(FSHKO-lyeh)

> I like math.
> Мне нравится математика.
> *(MNYE NRAH-vee-tsa ma-tee-MAH-tee-kuh.)*

> What is your name?
> Как тебя (вас) зовут?
> *(KAHK tee-BYA zah-VOOT?)*

teacher
учитель
(ooh-CHEE-tyel')

pencil
карандаш
(ka-rahn-DAHSH)

paper
бумага
(boo-MAH-guh)

computer
компьютер
(kahm-PYOO-tuhr)

desk
парта
(PAHR-tuh)

book
книга
(KNEE-guh)

MORE USEFUL WORDS

I like science.
Мне нравится наука.
(MNYE NRAH-vee-tsa nah-OO-kuh.)

I like art.
Мне нравится искусство.
(MNYE NRAH-vee-tsa ees-KOOHS-tvuh.)

I like music.
Мне нравится музыка.
(MNYE NRAH-vee-tsa MOO-zy-kuh.)

I like reading.
Мне нравится чтение.
(MNYE NRAH-vee-tsa CHTYE-nee-ye.)

Can I please go to the bathroom?
Можно выйти в туалет?
(MOZH-nuh VYJ-tee ftoo-ah-LYET?)

Please help me.
Пожалуйста, помогите мне.
(pah-ZHAH-loo-stah pah-ma-GHEE-tye MNYE.)

My name is _____.
Меня зовут _____.
(mee-NYA zah-VOOT _____.)

student
ученик
(ooh-chee-NEEK)

pen
ручка
(ROOCH-kuh)

homework
домашнее задание
(dah-MAHSH-nee-ye za-DAH-nee-ye)

At the Park
В парке
(FPAR-kyeh)

Let's play!
Давайте играть!
(dah-VAHJ-tyeh ee-GRAT'!)

sky
небо
(NYE-buh)

friend
друг
(DROOK)

soccer ball
футбольный матч
(food-BOL'-nyj MAHCH)

bird
птица
(PTEE-tsuh)

MORE USEFUL WORDS

game
игра
(ee-GRAH)

sports
спорт
(SPORT)

sun
солнце
(SOHN-tsye)

swing
качаться
(ka-CHAH-tsuh)

clouds
облака
(ahb-lah-KAH)

playground
детская площадка
(DYETS-kah-yah pla-SH'AHT-kuh)

slide
кататься с горки
(ka-TAH-tsuh ZGOHR-keeh)

water
вода
(va-DAH)

pond
пруд
(PROOT)

flower
цветок
(tsvee-TOHK)

duck
утка →
(OOT-kuh)

13

Around Town
По городу
(pah GO-rah-doo)

library
библиотека
(beeb-leeh-ah-TYEH-kuh)

LIBRARY

firefighter
пожарник
(pah-ZHAHR-neek)

Excuse me.
Извините.
(eez-veeh-NEEH-tyeh.)

woman
женщина
(ZHEHN-sh'ee-nuh)

man
мужчина
(moozh-CHEE-nuh)

police officer
полицейский
(pah-lee-tsyej-skeej)

street
улица
(OOH-lee-tsuh)

airplane
самолёт
(sah-mah-LYOT)

office
офис
(OH-fees)

building
здание
(ZDAH-nee-yeh)

bus
автобус
(ahf-TOH-boos)

CITY BUS

MORE USEFUL WORDS

train
поезд
(POH-eest)

truck
грузовик
(grooh-zah-VEEK)

stop
остановиться
(ah-stah-nah-VEE-tsa)

go
идти
(eet'-TEEH)

How much does an apple cost?
Сколько стоит одно яблоко?
(SKOL'-kuh STOH-eet ahd-NOH YAHB-lah-kuh?)

head
голова
(gah-lah-VAH)

body
тело
(TYEH-luh)

hand or arm
рука
(roo-KAH)

floor
этаж
(eeh-TAHSH)

foot
ступня
(stoop-NYAH)

leg
нога
(na-GAH)

MORE USEFUL WORDS

please
Пожалуйста
(pah-ZHAH-loo-stuh)

Thank you!
Спасибо!
(spah-SEE-buh!)

You are welcome!
Не за что!
(NE-zah-shtuh!)

How are you?
Как дела?
(kahg-dee-LAH?)

I am well.
Хорошо.
(khah-rah-SHOH.)

17

My Birthday Party
Мой День Рождения
(MOJ DYEN' razh-DYEH-nee-yah)

grandmother
бабушка
(BAH-boosh-kuh)

grandfather
дедушка
(DYEH-doosh-kuh)

I am six years old.
Мне шесть лет.
(MNYE SHYEST' LYET.)

brother
брат
(BRAHT)

sister
сестра
(sees-TRAH)

cake
торт
(TOHRT)

MORE USEFUL WORDS

one один *(ah-DEEN)*	eleven одиннадцать *(ah-DEE-nah-tsut')*
two два *(DVAH)*	twelve двенадцать *(dvee-NAH-tsut')*
three три *(TREE)*	thirteen тринадцать *(tree-NAH-tsut')*
four четыре *(chee-TY-ree)*	fourteen четырнадцать *(chee-TYR-nah-tsut')*
five пять *(PYAT')*	fifteen пятнадцать *(peet-NAH-tsut')*
six шесть *(SHYEST')*	sixteen шестнадцать *(shyes-NAH-tsut')*
seven семь *(SYEM')*	seventeen семнадцать *(seem'-NAH-tsut')*
eight восемь *(VOH-syem)*	eighteen восемьнадцать *(vah-seem'-NAH-tsut')*
nine девять *(DYEH-veet')*	nineteen девятнадцать *(dee-vyat-NAH-tsut')*
ten десять *(DYE-seet')*	twenty двадцать *(DVAH-tsut')*

19

Time for Dinner
Время
ужинать
(VRYEH-m'ah OO-zhee-nuht')

bread
хлеб
(KHLEHP)

stove
плита
(plee-TAH)

pot
кастрюля
(kahs-TRYOO-lyah)

I am hungry (male).
Я голоден.
(YA GOH-lah-dyen.)

I am hungry (female).
голодна.
(YA gah-lahd-NAH.)

glass
стакан
(stah-KAHN)

rice
рис
(REES)

meat
мясо
(MYA-suh)

plate
тарелка
(tah-RYEHL-kuh)

fork
вилка
(VEEL-kuh)

knife
нож
(NOHSH)

spoon
ложка
(LOHSH-kuh)

At Night
Ночью
(NOH-chyoo)

Today is Friday!
Сегодня пятница!
(see-VOHD-nyah PYAHT-nee-tsa!)

Yesterday was Thursday.
Вчера был четверг.
(fcheeh-RAH BYL cheet-VYERK.)

Tomorrow is Saturday.
Завтра будет суббота.
(ZAHF-truh BOO-deet soo-BOH-tuh.)

Good night!
Спокойной ночи!
(spah-KOY-nahj NOH-chee!)

bathtub
ванна
(VAHN-nuh)

I am tired! (masculine)
Я устал!
(YA oos-TAHL!)

I am tired! (feminine)
устала!
(YA oos-TAH-luh!)

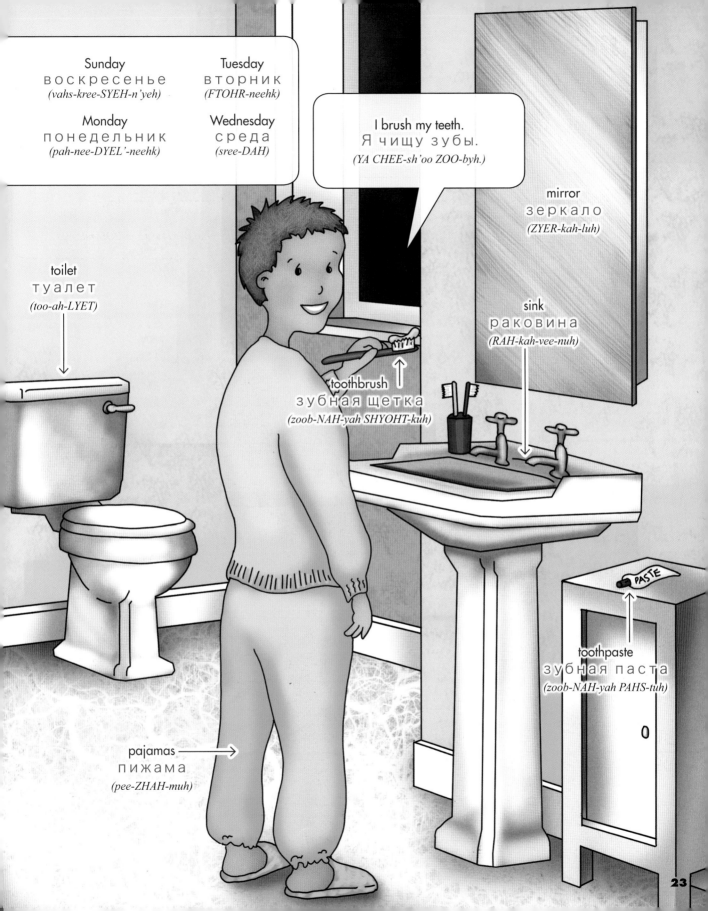

MORE USEFUL WORDS

Yes
Да
(DAH)

No
Нет
(NYET)

ten
десять
(DYE-seet')

twenty
двадцать
(DVAH-tsut')

thirty
тридцать
(TREE-tsut')

forty
сорок
(SOH-ruhk)

fifty
пятьдесят
(pee-dee-SYAHT)

sixty
шестьдесят
(sheez-dee-SYAHT)

seventy
семьдесят
(SYEM'-dee-syaht)

eighty
восемьдесят
(VOH-seem-dee-syaht)

ninety
девяносто
(dee-vee-NOH-stuh)

one hundred
сто
(STOH)

January
январь
(yeen-VAHR')

February
февраль
(fee-VRAHL')

March
март
(mahrt)

April
апрель
(ah-PRYEHL')

May
май
(mahy)

June
июнь
(ee-YOON')

July
июль
(ee-YOOL')

August
август
(AHV-goost)

September
сентябрь
(seen-TYAHBR')

October
октябрь
(ahk-TYAHBR')

November
ноябрь
(nah-YAHBR')

December
декабрь
(dee-KAHBR')

winter
зима
(zee-MAH)

spring
весна
(vees-NAH)

summer
лето
(LYEH-tuh)

fall
осень
(OH-seen')

good-bye!
Пока! До
свидания!
(pah-KAH! dah-svee-DAH-nee-yah!)